T0083670

Readings in World Literature

READINGS IN WORLD LITERATURE

Srikanth Reddy

OMNIDAWN PUBLISHING

RICHMOND, CALIFORNIA

2012

Cover photo by Jon Bobby Benjamin
Cover and Interior Design by Cassandra Smith

Typefaces: Didot LT Std and Adobe Garamond Pro

Printed on Glatfelter 55# B18 Antique

Published by Omnidawn Publishing, Richmond, California
www.omnidawn.com   (510) 237-5472   (800) 792-4957
10 9 8 7 6 5 4 3 2
978-1-890650-64-3

for Gopala Krishna Pennepalli

Time is a great teacher, they say. The pity of it is, she kills all her pupils.

-Berlioz, *Letters*

1   In the dismal, inky, and unprofitable research of a recent
leave of absence, I came across an inscription on a historical prism of
Assurbanipal which I found to be somewhat disquieting. Of an enemy
whose remains he had abused in a manner that does not bear repeating
here, this most violent and scholarly of Mesopotamian kings pronounces

I made him more dead than he was before.

(Prism A *Beiträge zum Inschriftenwerk*
Assurbanipals ed. Borger [Harrassowitz
1996] 241)

Prisms of this sort were often buried in the foundations of government
buildings and therefore intended to be read by gods but not men.
Somewhere in the maze of carrels and stacks I thought I could hear a
low dial tone humming without end. In Assurbanipal's library there is
a poem, written on clay, which corrects various commonly held errors
regarding the world of the dead. Contrary to the accounts of Mu Lian,
Odysseus, and Kwasi Benefo, for example, it is not customarily permitted
to visit the underworld. No, the underworld visits you.

2   Tunneling through sleep, the underworld visits a secondary character, sometimes described as the protagonist's double. Closing the door to the dream behind him, he notices that the inside bolt is thick with dust. He passes a heap of discarded crowns. The inmates, their mouths stained with clay, are suited in feathers. At the end of the corridor, he arrives at a registration desk:

> [There was] the queen of the underworld,
>   the goddess Ereškigal.
> Before her crouched [Bēlet]-Sēri, the clerk
>   of the underworld,
> holding [a tablet], reading aloud in her
>   presence.
>
> [She raised] her head. She saw me.
> "[Who was] it fetched this man here?
> [Who was it] brought [*this fellow*] here?"
>
> (*Babylonian Gilgamesh Epic* ed. A.R.
> George [Oxford 2003] 645)

Cuneiform tablets describing the Mesopotamian House of Dust frequently refer to a clerk who must enter the names of those scheduled to die each day. Little is known of this indefatigable figure. First, she has only one inexhaustible theme. Second, she writes for an ideal reader, the lady of the dead, who perpetually tears at her hair with fingers "like pickaxes." Third, she writes in a timeless form which allows for considerable prosodic variation en route to a fixed conclusion.

3   Some fragments from Assurbanipal's library may have fallen
from an upper story as the royal palace burned, while others were fractured
by weather, the plough, war, or archaeology itself. In the twilight of the last
millennium, however, one buoyant Assyriologist predicted that the holes
in this poem "will undoubtedly be filled by further discoveries of tablets
in the ruin-mounds of Mesopotamia" (insert citation here). But there are
so many holes—the hole in which the hero and his friend pray for safe
passage to the cedar forest, the hole containing an account of the friend's
pitiable death throes, the hole where the grave used to be—I'm afraid
recent developments in the region make Professor George's prognostication
less than likely. For the time being this house of dust, older than Hades, is
in pieces all over creation.

4   Already it is beginning to seem that I cannot avoid the subject of this nation's interminable occupation of the Republic of Iraq. But I would have preferred to write something along the lines of a poetic essay on comparative underworlds. For the past few years I have taught an introductory course titled "Readings in World Literature" which has generally proven to be a disappointment both to myself and to the students, some in headscarves, some occasionally dressed in fatigues, who have registered for this seminar in order to satisfy their Humanities requirement:

> It confirmed my hatred of epics and reaffirmed my faith that I will never study medieval literature.

> The instructor is fairly intelligent and enthusiastic about his brand of writing, but is unreceptive, even intolerant, of anything that is not a poem or a poem in prose form.

> Made me question the value of higher learning. It can so easily become detached from real life.

> (https://evaluations-uchicago-edu/evaluation.olcourseid=16882)

I thought that by writing about teaching I might learn something. There would be assignments, a midterm, and a final examination, followed by some sort of internal unraveling and the sound of snow falling on rooftops at night. I needed to find my footing in the order of things. And because I know almost nothing about the world, I decided to work my way up from below.

5   RWL 1100. *Introduction to the Underworld.* [Cross-listed with Comp Lit]. In this course, students will be ferried across the river of sorrow, subsist on a diet of clay, weigh their hearts against a feather on the infernal balance, and ascend a viewing pagoda in order to gaze upon their homelands until emptied of all emotion. Texts will include the Egyptian *Book of the Dead*, the Tibetan *Book of the Dead*, the Mayan *Book of the Dead*, the Ethiopian *Book of the Dead*, and Muriel Rukeyser's *Book of the Dead*. The goals of the course are to acquaint students with the posthumous regimes which entrench the division of humankind in perpetuity, and to help them develop the communication skills that are crucial for success in today's global marketplace.

All readings in English. Requirements include the death of the student, an oral presentation, and a 20-page final paper.

6   A jealous despot, writing, too, can make you more dead than you were before. In a letter to a fiancée he never married, Kafka touches upon this state of affairs:

> What I need for my writing is seclusion, not
> 'like a hermit,' that would not be enough, but
> like the dead. Writing, in this sense, is a sleep
> deeper than that of death, and just as one
> would not and cannot tear the dead from their
> graves, so I must not and cannot be torn away
> from my desk at night.
>
> (*Letters to Felice* eds. Heller and Born
> [Schocken 1973] 279)

I sometimes caution my students against quoting other writers in their poems. "You don't want the most memorable lines in your work to belong to somebody else," I profess. But really I think it has more to do with some sort of limbic taboo about inviting the dead to enter one's study. Our standard editorial versions of several Mesopotamian poems, including *The Epic of Gilgamesh*, were originally redacted by an ancient class of priestly exorcists. Kafka was a kind of exorcist, too. Here is his incantation:

> One can never be alone enough when one
> writes.
>
> There can never be enough silence
> surrounding one who writes.
>
> Even night is not night enough.
>
> (*LF* 156, redaction mine)

7   I promised my wife that I would call Dr. Song today. After putting the baby down for her nap and slipping outside for a smoke, I lifted the receiver. The sound it emitted, which I have heard without pause countless times before, seemed to me otherworldly now, like somebody's finger playing upon the wet rim of a crystal bowl in a derelict theater before the wars. I can't say how long I stood there listening. It may have been seconds or seasons. The rings of Saturn kept turning in their groove. For reasons I do not fully understand—my unit on Dante was not scheduled until the following quarter—I dialed 1-800-INFERNO, and, before the first ring, a woman's voice answered in heavily accented English: "Is it you?" "I think so," I replied. Outside my window, the honey locusts sprinkled their pale spinning leaves. Focusing on one as it fell seemed to slow the general descent. "Oh creature, gracious and good / traversing the dusky element to visit us / who stained the world with blood," the woman recited as if reading, against her will, from a prepared text. I could hear rain trickling in a gutter spout on the other end of the line. "Please remove my name from your list," I said, and placed the receiver back in its cradle.

8   While outlining the requirements for our first critical essay of the term, I notice a hand rising, tentatively, like a snake-charmer's serpent, in the classroom's farthest corner.

"What if I'm ideologically opposed to revision?" asks the red-headed boy in a *New Slaves* t-shirt.

A city bus unloads its pageantry just outside the window. A handful of sparrows erupts from the equestrian statue on the quad. I remember Sun Tzu's advice to humanities instructors, which I review on index cards on the eve of each new term: "Hold out baits to entice the enemy. Feign disorder, and crush him."

"What exactly is your ideology?" I ask, stroking my beard.

"I'm a Zen Naxalite crypto-Objectivist," replied my interlocutor. "How about you?"

Removing the stray bran flake that I have discovered, too late, lodged in my beard, I have no choice but to improvise: "Pro-recycling, anti-genocide?"

A voice from beyond my peripheral vision says, "You're nothing but a pseudo-Kantian neoliberal mirage with meta-narcissistic tendencies."

"No, I'm not."

"Yes, you are."

"No, I'm not."

"Yes, you are."

9   A window onto the purgatorial cosmology of late-imperial China may be found on page 26 of Léon Wieger's *Folklore Chinois Moderne* (Sienhsien: Imprimerie de la Mission Catholique, 1909). Throughout his forty years of residence in the Celestial Empire, this unsung Jesuit Sinologist labored to dismantle what he once called "the whole unbearable grid into which we have forcibly cantonized God's children." Contemporary Anglophone readers, however, must do without an English version of Father Wieger's *Folklore*. "I don't want any more English translations," he writes in a letter to his superiors, dated 3 February 1929. "English benefits Protestants, and it is not my goal to do so." Thus the strange tale of Chen from Hou-tcheou-fou remains largely unknown in this land. But if you will pardon my French, which is damnable (*adj.* 1. execrable; worthy of condemnation [now regarded as vulgar or profane]. *Obs. rare.*) indeed, I thought I might venture the following rough English rendition for purposes of instruction.

Draft only; please do not circulate.

10   In Hou-tcheou-fou, the magistrate's assistant Chen was taking a nap in his study. Suddenly a spirit appeared and beckoned to him. It led him down a path hidden by rustling thickets of bamboo to a clearing where, on a pedestal, an enormous mirror waited in the moonlight. "Regard what you once were," intoned the spirit.

Looking into the mirror, Chen saw a man in a quaint cap and scarlet shoes, dressed like a scholar from the past.

"Now see," said the spirit, "what you were in the life before that one." Chen looked again into the mirror and saw a high official in old Ming costume: black cap, red robe, belt with jade buckle, black boots.

Just then a servant entered the clearing, prostrated himself before Chen, and said to him, "Don't you recognize me? I was your servant in Ta-t'oung-fou, but then again, that was over two hundred years ago." With that said, he handed a scroll to Chen.

"Qu'est ceci?" Chen asked.

"Voici," said the servant.

11   "During the reign of Kia-tsing (1522-1566) in the Ming dynasty, you were called Wang Hsiu, and under that name you held the military governorship of Ta-t'oung-fou. You have been summoned here today with regard to an affair from those times," said the dead factotum. "Five hundred lost souls have lodged a complaint with the underworld magistrate Wenn-sinn-wang. They were rebels who had surrendered after the defeat of Liou-ts'i and laid down their arms. You are to be questioned about the cause of their death. But I, your loyal servant of yore, remember that those men were slain against your wishes. It was General X who slit their throats. [I have altered the order of sentences here for purely literary reasons—*trans*]. You see, General X wanted to exterminate these brutes, to prevent them from rising up once again. But you had written him a letter to dissuade him from such a course of action. That is the document which I have come to return to you. It will acquit you."

12   Upon hearing his tale, affairs from long ago began to infiltrate Chen's memory, although in a disordered and cloudy fashion. He thanked his old domestic.

"Would you prefer to travel on foot or in a litter?" inquired the spirit.

"Who ever heard of a high functionary trudging about on foot?" the servant exclaimed.

Just then an ornate palanquin with two stout porters hoisted Chen off the ground. After a journey of many days and nights, he arrived at a palace. In the great chamber sat a man with a white beard, dressed in royal apparel. A bailiff in violet robe and black cap, holding a massive registry, called the defendant Wang Hsiu.

"Please call to the stand General X," said Chen, "for it was he who undertook this mischief entirely on his own initiative."

The bailiff called General X. At once a towering figure, wearing full armor over his uniform, emerged from an alcove. Chen recognized his ancient colleague. The judge interrogated him at length, then summoned Wang Hsiu.

Chen advanced, folded his hands, and bowed deeply.

13   Our nanny called in sick yesterday, and I stayed home with the baby, watching a tree squirrel tuck twigs and trash into her wreck of a nest outside the kitchen window, instead of continuing with my translation.

"I love eyebrows," announced Mira, crumpling her bib. "I love napkins. I love upstairs."

On the radio, a program about efforts to restore various archaeological sites in and around the provincial capital of Al Hillah, where the ancient Mesopotamian city of Babylon once stood.

Speaking through an interpreter, a government official described how the 2600-year-old paving stones of the ancient city's Processional Way had been crushed under the treads of M1 Abrams tanks. Concertina wire lined extensive trenches dug for firing positions. A heliport had been constructed in the ruins. The remains of a ziggurat which some scholars believe may be the original site of the Tower of Babel, however, appeared to be spared for the time being.

"I love flowers. I love fire," Mira continued. "I love foreheads, too."

At some point in the day, Dr. Song left a message for me, but I couldn't make anything of it. Later that evening, I looked in the bathroom mirror to see if I could discern any trace of infractions from a previous life. All I could see, though, was the chipped and tarnished surface of the mirror itself, flickering almost imperceptibly. I looked again. This time, to my relief, I saw a man dressed like a scholar from the recent past: vintage cardigan, thinning hair, an untenured affect of worry beyond repair.

I love forks. I love giraffes. I love handles, too.

14   Melanoma, from the ancient Greek verb *melaino*, to blacken, combined with the nominalizing suffix -*ma*, which indicates process or action. Hence *pragma*, action or occurrence, from *pratto*, to do, or *poiema*, poem, from *poieo*, to make.

These days it is obligatory for survivors' narratives to muse upon the etymologies of their various illnesses and medical treatments. It lends grandeur to the experience of leafing through *Redbook* in an empty examination room while dressed in a paper gown that won't draw closed around the back.

But I cannot refrain from wondering at how a description, black, becomes an action, to blacken, which in turn becomes a thing, melanoma, a darkening. There is a whole grammar and metaphysics to this black traffic. The root points backwards, to the Sanskrit *mala-*, dirt or filth, and forward to our modern English melancholy.

15   A Strasbourg physician in his preclerical existence, Father
Wieger was not above manipulating the Chinese mania for Western
medicine during his mission abroad. Upon arriving in Xian Xan, he
established a distribution center for European-style medicines labeled
with Chinese characters. Remedy number three, or "sponge water,"
came with the following instructions:

> When the vital spirit is diminished and close
> to disappearing, when the limbs are cold, when
> the eyes roll upwards, and the child can no
> longer weep, he is like a lamp that has run out
> of oil and is on the verge of going out. Other
> remedies will cease to have any effect on him,
> but this remedy will still work its effect. There
> is no longer cause for saying that nothing can
> be done, that you have no power to help.

> Directions for remedy number three:

> Take a cup of pure, luke-warm water, soak
> the sponge in it, then dribble the juice from
> the sponge over the forehead. To increase
> the power of this remedy, use it with number
> thirteen, stimulating seed.

The Chinese laborers who administered remedy number three to their
children had no way of knowing that "sponge water" was, in fact, holy
water. Instead of medical treatment, they were furnishing the sacrament
of baptism to their rapidly fading patients. "Even on the day he died,"
recalls Father H. Bernard, "Wieger delighted in reading the missionaries'
notes enumerating the thousands of dying children who had received the
sponge juice." (Material on Wieger here and elsewhere plagiarized from
Bresner and Gage "Fathers of Sinology" [Diogenes 178: 45/2] 116-7).

16   My little translation is losing steam, I'm afraid. So much has happened since I left poor Chen in the court of the infernal magistrate, the case now seems hopeless at best. All the back and forth about chain of command, culpability, and war crimes, in particular, is giving me no end of grief.

"You think you are quite innocent," the judge says to Chen, "because you wrote General X not to do it. But Ming law gives you more power over him than he has over himself."

[I hereby formally and personally apologize for the massacre of unnumbered indigenous men and women by imperial forces under the command of Gaius Suetonius Paulinus on the modern-day Isle of Anglesey during the Roman conquest of Britain in AD 60 or 61 as reported by Publius Cornelius Tacitus (*Annals* 14:30)—*trans*].

And yet "a whirlwind black as ink" rises from the ground, accompanied by a piercing whistle and an unbearable odor of blood. The skeletal victims of the massacre emerge from this vortex and bury their teeth in "l'ex-général X," leaving Chen both mortified and relieved.

[Here I officially deny all responsibility for the massacre of unnumbered Sauk and Fox families as they fled the guns of Captain Joseph Throckmorton across the Bad Axe River outside of Victory, WI on the 1st and 2nd of August 1832 as reported by wikipedia.org—*trans*].

"Misérables!" The judge pounds his desk and demands an explanation from these unruly wraiths. There is some more back and forth, ending with the referral of the two-centuries'-old case, which antedates this magistrate's jurisdiction, to a higher court, following some minor reprimands which I have not yet managed to decipher.

17   "The odds are good," Dr. Song tells me in his office. Still, he blinks too much as he answers my wife's questions about this perplexing case. Melanoma is exceedingly rare among individuals of my dusky extraction, and virtually nonexistent among younger members of this population. ("You're a medical miracle," joked one nurse before I went under. "But not the good kind"). At least my tests show no spread to the neighboring lymph nodes, which lowers the probability of dying within three years to roughly one in ten. Not bad odds. I resolve to not make too much of my condition in the days to come. But the complimentary brochure that I take from the rack as I exit the reception area says I mustn't make too little of it either. In this respect, my condition is not unlike the war. I don't want to make too much of it in my ambient transactional order. But I don't want to make too little of it either.

18   The judge ordered the spirit to accompany Chen home. They retraced their steps through the pathway hidden by bamboo, and emerged into the clearing with the mirror once more. There his old servant congratulated Chen on his acquittal.

"Come," said the spirit with a smile, "and see what you were in this life."

Chen looked in the mirror, and saw himself dressed as an assistant magistrate of the Tsing Dynasty.

"Now see what you are going to become."

At these words, Chen was so convulsed by horror that he awoke, bathed in great beads of sweat. He was stretched out in his study, his whole family weeping around him. Somebody told him that he had lain dead to the world all day and night, the area around his heart alone retaining some faint trace of human warmth.

Suspended at intervals throughout the court of the otherworldly judge, Chen had noticed a number of banners adorned with infernal maxims. He could remember none but the following:

The court of the dead makes exceptions for no one.

When the waters fall, the stones appear; thus everything is revealed in its time.

All is counted on the infinite abacus.

19   "Things are becoming a shade Eurocentric by this point in the syllabus, don't you think?"

It was New Slaves again, declaring an end to our de facto armistice of late. To make matters worse, the dial tone in my head had resurfaced, only now it sounded like nothing so much as a flat-lined EKG monitor.

"Sorry?"

"You can't just peddle orientalist esoterica mediated by quasi-poststructuralist translation practices in service of a faux-naïf globalizing logic," he continued, as if reading from an invisible grimoire. "That sort of vulgar cosmopolitanism merely facilitates the Western colonization of the underworld as a site of metaphysical alterity."

He had a point. "Fine," I said. "Can you think of someplace we might start over again?"

"That's your job, not mine."

The room had assumed the tenebrous gloom of a star chamber. The days were growing colder. I watched the clock on the classroom's far wall pulsing, mercifully, indifferently, toward the end of the period.

"There is always Xibalba," ventured a quiet girl to my left whose name I had yet to learn.

"Never been there," I said.

20   "My father likes to tell this story," said the quiet girl. "He heard it from an old woman in the forest while he was AWOL from the Guatemalan army."

People stopped packing away their books. Some who had stood up to leave sat down again.

"He wasn't cut out for marching all over the country burning down people's houses. He says the pay was a joke. It was dangerous work, too. One girl threw lime in his friend's eyes and blinded him for good. When the villagers didn't have machetes or stones on hand they would even throw chile in your face. So he ran away into the mountains and was lost there for weeks and weeks, maybe months, he doesn't know how long."

"How did he survive?" asked a Korean boy with a thick Boston accent.

"He lived on river snails and whatever else he could find in the forest. Finally he came across a village high in the clouds where the people knew nothing about the outside world. They grew everything in their gardens, plantains, pumpkins, maize, and beans, but they were so isolated they didn't have salt, only some kind of black stone that they used instead. To my father, it was wonderful. He says he still misses the taste."

21   In the doorway, students arriving for the next period's class were beginning to gather. Their instructor, a middle-aged graduate student in philosophy, peered at us expectantly though spectral spectacles.

"It was cold up there, so cold that his jaw ached at night, but an old Indian woman, a *chimán*, took him in, fed him, and before sending him on his way, she told him this story," said the girl. "One day the lords of Xibalba, One Death and Seven Death, heard two brothers playing ball noisily overhead, and summoned them for a match down below. The boys, whose father had been murdered by One Death and Seven Death long ago, floated across the river of blood on their blowguns and arrived in time for the contest. On successive nights their hosts lodged them in the House of Darkness, the House of Blades, and the House of Cold where it is forever snowing inside. Still the brothers played well, and could only be defeated by their own design.

At the conclusion of the games, One Death and Seven Death dug a pit oven and asked the boys to leap over it four times in celebration. But the brothers said 'Don't you think we recognize our own death?' and jumped right in. When the lords of Xibalba dumped their remains in the river, two fish with human faces appeared in the current and swam out of sight."

22   "The next day, a pair of vagabonds showed up in the neighborhood. People came from all corners of Xibalba to watch them perform. They would set fire to a house and with the wave of a hand restore it to its original condition. One extracted the other's still-beating heart and wrapped it in a leaf like a tamale, but the victim went on dancing."

The philosopher in the doorway tapped his wrist as if to say hurry up please it's time. Somebody slurped noisily from a water fountain in the hallway. The girl paid no mind.

"The lords of Xibalba got wind of these curious visitors, and summoned them to their court," she continued, addressing a darkening window. "'I absolutely insist that you burn down my home!' said One Death (or Seven Death, they were hard to tell apart). So the pair set fire to the house with all the dark gods crowded inside, yet none were touched by the flames.

After the entertainers had slain and brought back to life a dog, an innocent bystander, and one another by turns, One Death and Seven Death cried out in a frenzy, 'Do it to us! Sacrifice us!'

So the boys cut out the hearts of One Death and Seven Death. But they left those gods dead in the dust. Then they cursed the lords of the underworld, and from that day onward the people of this land no longer sacrificed each other to please the shades underfoot."

The room was dark by now. The quiet girl stood up to leave. Somebody turned on the overhead lights.

"Thank you," I said.

You never know what sort of hell a person is carrying inside.

23   On a summer day between the wars, the entrance to the
underworld appeared, briefly, in the seal pool at the zoological gardens of
the Bois de Boulogne. In order to film Enrico Rivero's passage through
the looking glass in *Le Sang d'un Poete*, Jean Cocteau constructed his
set at a 90-degree angle to the ground on this site, filming the following
sequence from a nearby rooftop:

> Mirror in full view. The poet plunges into the
> glass. The cry of a crowd at a fireworks display
> accompanies his disappearance.
>
> (We have substituted for the mirror a pool of
> water, turned the stage on its side, the chair
> nailed to the left. The camera shoots the scene
> looking down from above. The actor dives in.
> A quick cut to the room turned right side up
> as it was before puts an end to the illusion).
>
> (*Le Sang d'un Poète* [Éditions du Rocher 1957]
> 39, translator anonymous)

I view this sequence repeatedly in the dim gloom of the university's film
studies center—play, pause, reverse, play—in an idle attempt to freeze
the frame where mirror becomes pool, vertical becomes horizontal, and
the living dead. In the neighboring booth, a former student whose name
escapes me slouches, sullen in hoodie and headphones, before some sort
of ultraviolent hyperkinetic anime kaleidoscope. Life, death, reverse,
play. Before I know it, the viewing station has tilted precariously and
I am pitched headlong through the screen into a dark arctic element
unfathomable to man. Rivero descends, a lifeline of bubbles trailing from
his lips. I plunge after.

24   Dead and buried before I was born, Rivero sinks more swiftly
than I can dive, and, though my heart has slowed to one tenth of its
customary rate in order to conserve oxygen during my descent, he soon
vanishes into the pixellated depths.

A specimen jar floats by, lit from within, housing a nervous frog perched
on a leaf. The jar and its contents tumble into the darkness.

I pass an old woman with bone earrings, hunched before a loom. She has
nearly completed her Battle of Cannae. Spent horses kneel in their own
blood. In the foreground, an unfinished figure raises his shield to the rain
of black arrows. Smoke is woven throughout the composition to great
effect. The whole affair turns one last awkward somersault and recedes,
too, into the darkness.

A woebegone dog, mangy and emaciated, brings to mind the strange tale
of Mr. Liu, who could recall his past lives in some detail. A stray dog in a
previous existence, Liu was fully conscious that his own excrement had a
foul essence, and yet its fragrance made his mouth water.

These and countless others do I encounter on my descent, too various to
tell. Still, I descend.

Sunk into the deep sea bed like a page awaiting translation, a wrecked
tanker oxidizes below. Under the deck lives a moribund youth with
literary aspirations, dressed as a bureaucratic flunky from turn of the
century Prague. I can hear him down there, bolt upright in his cot, his
breathing labored, as if forever just woken from a nightmare.

25   When I lift my head, a stubborn filament of saliva tethers my lower lip to the console. My old student is gone, the screening room evacuated of every last soul save the attendant, who watches my fumbling from behind her taped-together copy of the Penguin *Upanishads* with studied disregard. Back home, I look up the name of that drowned ship. Somehow it sounds familiar. I learn that it relates to how a person arrives at knowledge through memory. In the Platonic sense, it suggests the recollection of ideas which the soul knew in a previous life. In a clinical sense, it is the full medical history as told by a medical or psychiatric patient. In immunology, it is a strong immune response. Anamnesis. It appears to be one of those words that won't take death for an answer.

26   Yesterday the doorbell rang while I was emptying the dishwasher. I undid the chain and opened the door to find a bloody skeleton on our front steps. It shifted its weight uneasily from one foot to the other. Clouds scrolled across the sky in rapid formation.

"Are you lost?" I asked.

"They said I had to come," said my visitor.

"Who are they? Who do you mean?"

Inside its socket, the left eye twitched, but there was no answer. A black and green beetle stumbled across the welcome mat.

"Where is your family?" I asked. "Where are your friends?"

"I am a resident alien among both the living and the dead," intoned the little system of bones. "I'm not at home with human beings or corpses."

I might have misheard that last bit. Some kind of glitch in the jaw mechanism made the words hard to follow.

"Sorry, come again?" I asked. "I'm afraid I don't understand."

But by now I could see them approaching from every direction, some in the middle of the street, some angling across the neighbor's driveway, others emerging from the alley by the electric company's power shed— ghosts, zombies, ballerinas and worse—as if all a body needed was a flimsy little mask to trespass upon the lawns of the living.

27   "Monsters, monsters, everywhere," chanted a scarecrow, an oversized spider, and a sorry-looking robot who had taken up position at the bottom of the steps, "but none more monstrous than man."

My breath made a little ghost in the air. It rose and expired like steam from an uncovered manhole.

"Blasted by sub-zero winds, he flits across the grizzled sea, threading his way through swells that would gulp him down whole," continued my new friends, inching to the left with small, shuffling steps. "He wears down the oldest god, enduring Earth, unzipping her soil with his plough year after year, dragged along by the horses he breaks."

These were clearly the children of faculty members. Tootsie Rolls would be useless against them.

"The society of birds with their heads full of air, the beast's brutish tribe, the biomass swarming in the sea," they chanted in chorus, now shuffling to the right, "he scoops them all up in the convoluted nets he contrives and hauls them offstage."

Something had clamped itself onto my leg. I looked down, and there was Mira. "Die, die," she said, but I didn't take it personally. At this point in the historical development of her language, which my wife called Old Middle Baby Talk, "die" meant 1. a folded piece of absorbent material, usually paper or cloth, that is placed between a baby's legs and fastened at the waist, or 2. in the imperative mood, change my diaper.

"Meticulous man," said my visitors, holding out their empty sacks.

28   It is always never a good time for a full medical report on
Antigone. She is continually displaying new symptoms, new costumes,
new customs, new systems. To begin with, there is the lost *Antigone*
of Euripides. All that remains of her is a few scraps of text quoted by
Aristophanes in *The Frogs*. Later comes Hölderlin's *Antigonä* with her
mouth like a floodlight. Then Brecht's, with her mouth like a floodlight
whose bulb has burned out. In Japan, Antigone after Antigone sprang
up after the bomb. A Turkish Antigone speaks out for exploited cobalt
miners. The Yoruban Tegonni makes masks herself. All these Antigones,
however, suffer from the same burial disorder. They cannot tolerate the
thought of the dead among the living. Hence the corpse sprinkled with
dust at such great expense. Also, they cannot live among the dead. Thus
the noose in the cave.

29   Now and then I find myself scrolling through lists of the most recent fatalities online. A website called "Iraq Body Count," with a grim little image of an American stealth bomber dispensing its munitions at the top of the page, logs documented civilian deaths from violence in the form of a scarlet graph that calls to mind a medical chart of some patient's disordered brain activity. You can even download an IBC counter for your website or blog, though that seems like overkill to me. I never get far in these lists. I just dip in and out of them, not because it would be too painful to go on, but because it would not be painful enough. Wife of dead man (Al-Zahraa, east Mosul). Sister-in-law of dead man (Al-Zahraa, east Mosul). Daughter of dead man (Al-Zahraa, east Mosul). Perhaps if the Antigones at Iraq Body Count could include a thumbnail image of each victim, or a few lines of verse in honor of the deceased, that might be helpful. Anyway I sprinkle some dust between subcommittee meetings and visits to the Xerox machine in this manner.

30   On the last day of class, I ask my students, who, like their instructor, have no Latin and less Greek, to render Antigone's grave wedding song into modern English. But first, some fresh oatmeal cookies I purchased for the occasion. Little hammers in the classroom's radiators begin to pound out an alien meter as I write the opening line on the blackboard:

> horat' em' ō gas patrias politai

There is a brief period of universal scribbling, and an Uzbek premed in a deconstructed peasant blouse raises her hand. "Whore Adam, oh gasp at tree as Pa lit high," she recites. A discussion of the theological reverberations of this effort quickly fizzles out. Outside, the first snow of the year descends so softly that it seems to fall upward. We work our way through the song with a growing sense of unreality. New Slaves discovers the full visible spectrum of vowels in *aeliou*, genitive masculine singular of the sun. Ancient pipes whistle a faint accompaniment under the floorboards. They are not learning. I am not teaching. Hades, who tucks everybody into bed in the end, is escorting us, still breathing, to the shore of the River Akheron. There is no ceremony. No wedding song sings us down the aisle. Nonetheless, we shall marry Akheron.

31 The river of fire, according to certain dead Greeks, feeds into the river of pain.

From the river of pain spring two rivers: the river of lamentation and the river of hate.

The river of forgetting is a separate affair entirely.

At the sight of sinners approaching, the Vaitarani seethes "like butter in a frying pan," says the Garuda Purana.

Ksaranadi, in Sanskrit, is the river of ash.

As the sun god Ra floats down the river of the hidden chamber, his head is exchanged for that of a ram.

The vessel, too, changes shape underfoot—serpent boat, one-eyed boat, funeral boat, boat towed by jackals—as it journeys toward the third hour of the night.

The sun cannot step into the same boat twice.

To my knowledge, the Zoroastrian river of tears has no name.

Those for whom much lamentation is made find it swollen with tears and difficult to cross, attests Arda Viraf.

The passage is easier for those who go unwept.

32   There are two ways to exit the land of the dead. You or I might plan our escape through the portal of horn. False dreams, however, leave through an ivory gate:

> Sunt geminae Somni portae, quarum altera fertur
> cornea, qua veris facilis datur exitus umbris;
> altera candenti perfecta nitens elephanto,
> sed falsa ad caelum mittunt insomnia Manes.

> (*Aeneid* ed. H.R. Fairclough [Loeb 1916]
> 604).

Why, then, does the protagonist, whose armored weight makes Charon's skiff groan underfoot, depart through the exit reserved for airy illusions? A river of ink has poured into this centuries-old question. When I close my eyes, the river appears. Like a cormorant caught in an oil spill, blind Borges wades out of the shallows in goggles and flippers. He spreads his towel beside me on the current's moving edge. "It just goes to show," he declares, citing his lecture on nightmares, "that what we deem reality is in fact fiction." A cloud like a fist rotates slowly overhead. I reach into the black stream and come up with my hands full of ticking crickets. What we deem fact is in reality fiction. What we deem reality is in fiction fact. What we deem fiction is in fact reality. And so on. I have never been good at dead languages. Even the living ones feel dead to me. The only theory that makes any sense is the one where the protagonist never returns.

33   The day after the blizzard, I emerge with my shovel to dig an igloo for Mira. The snow seems lit by a cornflower glow from within, as if there were a whole sky cached underneath. "Die Nacht unter dem Salze," goes Hölderlin's Sophokles. The night under the salt. Earlier this morning the government unveiled new procedures for deciding the fate of those foreign souls incarcerated in our name. I let the thought pass. As I dig, I am aware of an absence of sensation where the dissolving sutures vanished long ago. Song says it's a matter of time before feeling returns. I let this thought, too, pass. My wife tows Mira, an unstable weather system unto herself, around the yard on a blue plastic sled, while I heap up a perimeter. Our daughter is, it seems, still too little to thrill with a house made of snow. Later we will take turns crawling inside, coaxing her to join us for hot chocolate or a story, but she balks at the entrance, quizzical, lit from behind in her parka and toque. Crouching there in that hollow, I feel nearly at home, for reasons quite beyond me.

Acknowledgments

My thanks to the curators Kira Wisniewski and William Bert, who commissioned this poem for the exhibit "Call + Response" at the Hamiltonian Gallery in Washington, DC. I am grateful, too, to the artist Jon Bobby Benjamin, whose sculptural response to this poem for that exhibit appears on the cover of this book. Time and space for writing was provided by a fellowship at the Franke Institute for the Humanities; I would like to express my appreciation to the founders, director, staff, and fellows at the Institute for making this work possible. Finally, the friends, colleagues, and family who have lent their generous support to this project are too numerous to name here. But Ilya Kaminsky, Daniel Beachy-Quick, and Sally Keith all deserve a special measure of gratitude for their insightful comments on various stages of the work, as does, as always, Suzanne Buffam.

PHOTO BY SUZANNE BUFFAM

Srikanth Reddy is the author of two books of poetry—*Facts for Visitors* (2004) and *Voyager* (2011)—and a book-length collaboration with Daniel Beachy-Quick, titled "Conversities." A graduate of the Iowa Writer's Workshop and Harvard University's doctoral program in English, Reddy is an assistant professor at the University of Chicago.